Improve your STUDY SKILLS

Susan Baing

OXFORD

253 Normanby Road, South Melbourne, Victoria 3205, Australia

Oxford University Press is a department of the University of Oxford. It furthers the University's objective of excellence in research, scholarship, and education by publishing worldwide in

Oxford New York

Auckland Cape Town Dar es Salaam Hong Kong Karachi Kuala Lumpur Madrid Melbourne Mexico City Nairobi New Delhi Shanghai Taipei Toronto

With offices in

Argentina Austria Brazil Chile Czech Republic France Greece Guatemala Hungary Italy Japan Poland Portugal Singapore South Korea Switzerland Thailand Turkey Ukraine Vietnam

First published 2002
Reprinted 2007, 2009, 2010, 2016 (D)

ISBN 978 0 19 551589 3.

Edited by Kate Deutrom and Paige Amor
Text and cover designed by Aileen Taylor
Illustrated by Melissa Webb
Typeset by Promptset Pty Ltd
Printed in Australia by Ligare Pty Ltd.

Contents

Overview—*Improve Your Study Skills*

Dictionary skills

Reading skills

Writing skills

Examination skills

Please use your Oxford University Press Dictionary when required.

Answer all questions in your own exercise book.

To the student

You will find four important study skills in this book. They are dictionary skills, reading skills, writing skills and skills to use for exam time. All of the skills in this book will help you to study more successfully.

There is some information about each skill and some exercises for you to do. To improve your dictionary, reading, writing and exam skills, you must practice the skills in this book every time you use a dictionary, read a book, write a letter, essay or story and every time you sit an exam. The only person who can help you to get better at using these skills is *yourself*. For example, there are some ideas in the reading section to help you read faster. If you want to read faster you have to use the ideas in the reading skills section every time you read.

To the teacher

This book outlines some skills that will help students improve their study skills. However, the skills that are presented must be reinforced and practiced continually to have an effect.

The information and exercises in each section provide an outline and some ideas. You can help students improve by giving them tasks that help them practice these skills. If the skills are used everyday in the classroom, you will soon see an increase in your students' skills. For example, students can practice the reading skills of skimming and scanning at the start of any reading task in any subject area.

Unit 1

How dictionary entries work

Here is a sample of a dictionary page to show you how the dictionary works.

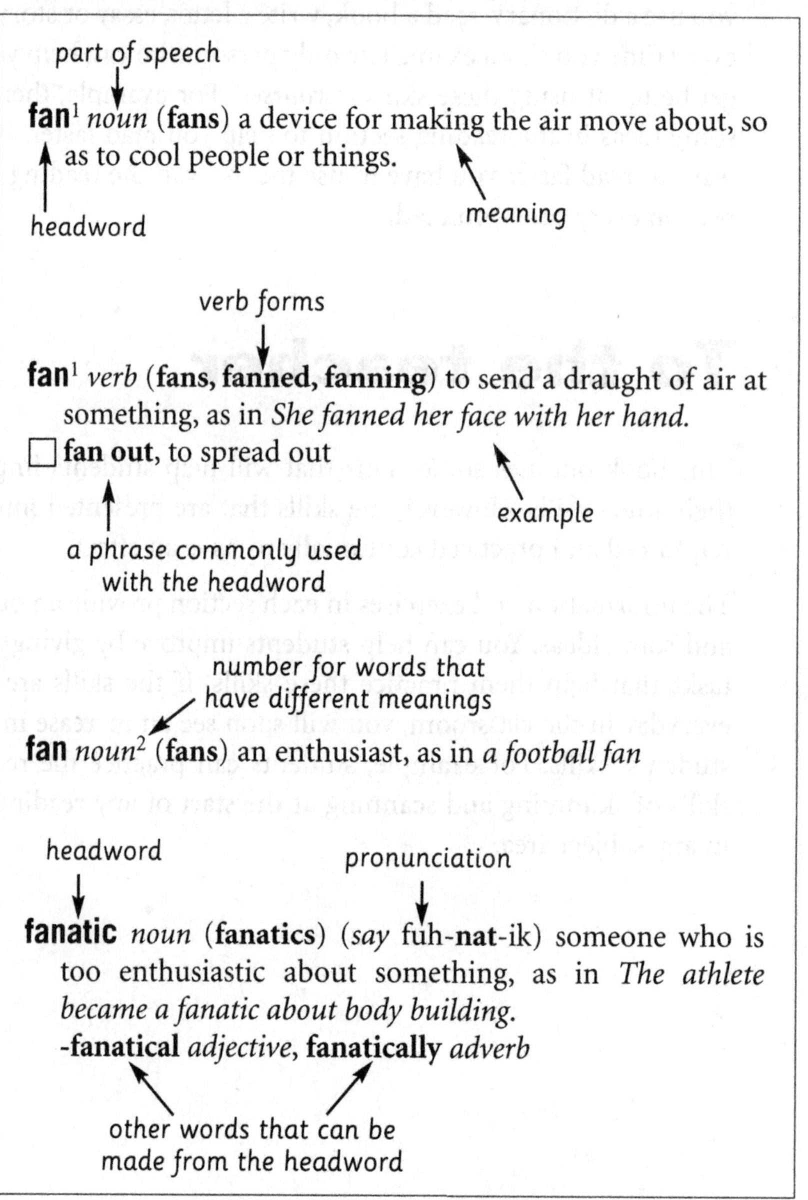

Activity A

Here are some more words from the same dictionary. Identify and write what each arrow points to.

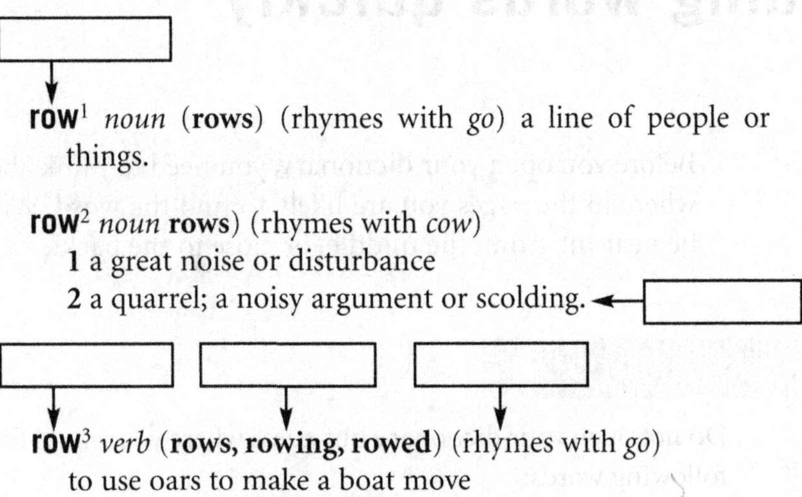

row[1] *noun* (**rows**) (rhymes with *go*) a line of people or things.

row[2] *noun* **rows**) (rhymes with *cow*)
1 a great noise or disturbance
2 a quarrel; a noisy argument or scolding.

row[3] *verb* (**rows, rowing, rowed**) (rhymes with *go*)
to use oars to make a boat move
-**rower** *noun*, **rowing-boat** *noun*

rowdy *adjective* (**rowdier, rowdiest**) noisy and disorderly.
-**rowdily** *adverb*, **rowdiness** *noun*, **rowdyism** *noun*

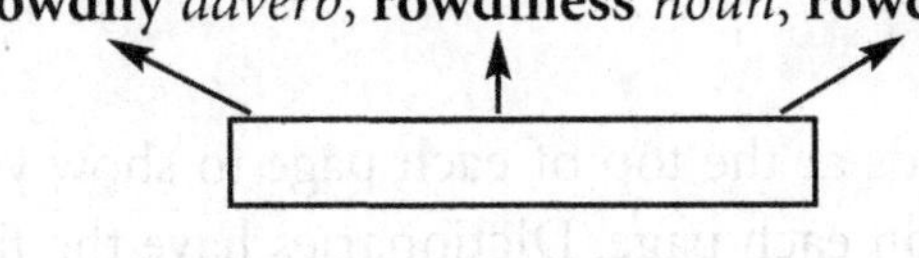

Activity B

Use your own dictionary to find out the following:

1 What can a sculpture be made of?
2 Is the word *fresh* an adjective, a noun or a verb?
3 What is the past tense of *swim*?
4 How do you spell the plural of the word *summons*?
5 How do you spell the *-ing* form of the verb *file*?
6 How are you told to say the word *chord*?
7 What noun can you form from the verb *reap*?
8 What new words are made by adding other words to *head*?

Unit 2

Finding words quickly

Before you open your dictionary, you need to think about where in the pages you are likely to find the word. Will it be near the front, the middle, or close to the back?

Activity A

Do not open your dictionary but guess where you would find the following words:

umpire, acupuncture, jagged, zodiac, credit.

Activity B

There are words at the top of each page to show you the words you will find on each page. Dictionaries have the first word and the last word on each page at the top of the page in thick letters. These words are called *guidewords*.

abrupt 2 **accentuate**	**accept** 3 **accurate**

Open your dictionary somewhere in the middle. What are the words at the top of that page? Find ten examples.

Activity C

Practise using the words at the top of the page to find individual words as quickly as possible. You should be able to find each one before you count to ten.

Example, *midst*—the guidewords are *microcomputer* and *milk*

Find the following words in the dictionary and write down the guidewords for the page:

removal	hollow
jockey	faint
adapt	medal
vault	meek
greed	square

Activity D

Without looking at your dictionary, decide which of the following words would be between these guidewords found at the top of your dictionary's pages and write them down.

For example, if the guidewords for the page are *paper* and *password*, which of these words would be on that page:

paralysis (✓), press (x), pass (✓), past (x)

Now do these:

splash/squaw
squad, spy, stain, spaceman, starve, spotlight

tag/tax
taxi, tea, task, talk, tadpole

changeable/childish
chew, charity, category, change, chieftain

Activity E

Look in your dictionary for words beginning with these letters:

1 A but _ _ _ is a fastener sewn on clothes.
2 To ins _ _ _ is to be very firm in asking or saying something.
3 A pe _ _ _ _ is a small round stone.
4 A reg _ _ _ is a part of a country.
5 To stru _ _ _ _ is to move your whole body to get free.

Unit 3

Using the dictionary

We use the dictionary to check the meanings of words we use.

Activity A

Look up the meaning of these words in the dictionary and match them with the words in the box:

squander beaker bungalow elastic
hour-glass nil abacus

cup	house	nothing	waste
	counting	stretch	time

Activity B

Some words are spelt the same but have very different meanings. The dictionary uses raised numbers (^{1}) after the word to show this.

Example:

bay[1] *noun* (**bays**) a place where the shore curves inwards

bay[2] *noun* (**bays**) a compartment or area especially marked off, as in *parking bay*; *loading bay*

bay[3] *adjective* a dark reddish-brown colour, as in *a bay horse*

Find the following words in the dictionary and write how many meanings there are:

1 ash

2 egg

3 fuse

4 refuse

5 row

6 scuttle

7 set

8 till

9 utter

10 will

Activity C

Some words have different meanings listed under them.

Example:

wantok *noun* (colloquial)

1 someone who speaks the same mother tongue.

2 a friend

Find the following words in the dictionary and write how many meanings are listed under them:

1 bind (verb)

2 bug (noun)

3 hop (verb)

4 horn (noun)

5 range (noun)

6 stack (noun)

7 test (noun)

8 warm (adjective)

9 write (verb)

10 X-ray (noun)

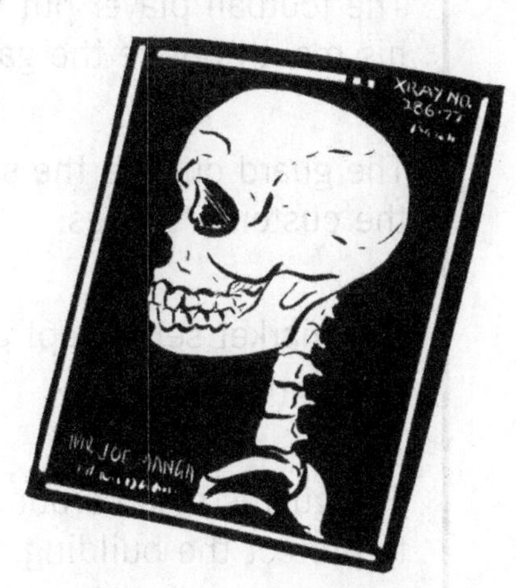

Activity D

1 Look up the word *test* [(*noun*) *tests*] in your dictionary. There are three meanings of *test*. Here are three sentences using *test*. Match the word and the number showing the meaning.

The doctor gave the girl a blood test for malaria.	1
Papua New Guinea played a test against Australia.	2
The teacher gave us some practice tests to do before our assessment test.	3

2 Look up the word *guard* [(*noun*) *guards*] in your dictionary. There are four meanings of *guard*. Here are four sentences using *guard*. Match the word and the number showing the meaning.

The football player put the mouth guard in his mouth before the game.	1
The guard outside the supermarket searched the customer's bags.	2
The market seller kept guard on her betel nut very carefully.	3
The guards stood around the police station to protect the building.	4

Activity E

Look up each of the following words in the dictionary. Find the number of the meaning. Write the explanation of the meaning. Write another sentence that shows that meaning clearly.

Example:

meaning 1 pay (*verb*)

1. to give money in return for something, as in *Have you paid for your lunch?*

2. [your sentence] *The coffee buyer paid the coffee seller for the coffee beans.*

1 meaning **1** bump (*noun*)
2 meaning **1** help (*verb*)
3 meaning **3** replace (*verb*)
4 meaning **5** side (*noun*)
5 meaning **3** grow (*verb*)

Activity F

Look up these special meanings under the words. They are shown by a small box □. Write the words and their meanings:

1 pat—a pat on the back
2 guard—guard against
3 afraid—I'm afraid
4 hand—at first hand

Unit 4

Why do you read? How do *you* read?

We read for different reasons and we read in different ways.

Activity A

Look at this list of reasons for reading and tick any of the kinds of reading that you do:

1 looking at the newspaper for reports on sports that interest you

2 reading a passage to answer questions the teacher gives you

3 reading a novel because you like to read

4 reading to find information you need for a social science project

5 reading a novel to answer questions the teacher gives you

Activity B

We read for two main reasons: for pleasure and to find information.

1 Go back to the list in Activity A. Put another tick if you think that kind of reading is for pleasure. Put a cross if you think that kind of reading is for information.

2 Write some more examples of when you read for pleasure, and when you read for information.

Activity C

Work with a partner. Watch each other while you read. Then talk about how your partner's eyes move. Follow these steps:

1 Hold the book or paper you are reading up in the air so that your partner can see your eyeballs.

2 Read silently the way you usually read.

3 Your partner will watch to see how your eyeballs move.

4 Now change over, so that you watch and your partner reads.

What did you see? Did your partner's eyeballs move smoothly, or did they jump?

You probably found that the eyeballs didn't move smoothly but jumped along the line of words. This is a slow way of reading. You need to train your eyes to look at more than one word at a time. That way you have less jumps and can read more quickly.

Here is an example to show you how you can train your eyes. Read these lines:

> Many countries in the Pacific have tropical rainforests, which are the home of many plants and animals.

If you read one word at a time, your eyes would jump seventeen times. Now look at the same lines and read in groups of words:

> (Many countries) (in the Pacific) (have tropical)
> (rainforests), (which are) (the home) (of many)
> (plants and animals).

Now your eyes should jump only eight times. You can practise this whenever you read.

Unit 5

Reading quickly—skimming and scanning

Have you ever thrown a flat stone across the water and watched it skim and skip? Have you watched a dragonfly looking for food in the water? This is what the reading techniques of *skimming* and *scanning* are like. Both skimming and scanning can help you read more quickly.

Skimming

Skimming is running your eyes quickly over a page to get a quick idea of what it is about. You use this way of reading to help you find information you want. It helps you to find information quickly. It means you do not have to read everything on a page.

Activity A

Read these two stories about students. Talk about what is different about the stories:

Kovave wanted to find out about agriculture in traditional times in Papua New Guinea. He found a book on Papua New Guinea agriculture. He opened the book at the first page and started to read. He read for many hours. When he found some information about traditional agriculture, he wrote it down in his notebook.

Leleani wanted to find out about agriculture in traditional times in Papua New Guinea. She found a book on Papua New Guinea agriculture. She opened the book at the first page and started to skim the pages. She read and skimmed for one hour. When she found some information about traditional agriculture, she wrote it down in her notebook.

Did you say this?

Both students found information on traditional agriculture, but Kovave wasted a lot of time. He read a lot of information he did not need. Lelani found the same information, but she used her reading time wisely.

Activity B

To do skimming properly, you need to be sure what information you are looking for.

Lelani and Kovave knew what to look for. They wanted to find out about agriculture in traditional times so they looked for the words *traditional* and *agriculture* together.

What words would you look for together to find out about these things? Some words are underlined to help you:

1 medicines that were used in traditional times

2 what different materials can be used to make bilums

3 where trade took place on the coast in traditional times

Activity C

When you want to find out information from a short passage you can use the skill of skimming. You skim to look for the *important words*. The important words are mostly verbs and nouns.

Read this summary of a newspaper article. Many words have been left out, but you can still understand the article because the important words are still there:

> **SIX ESCAPE IN CRASH**
>
> Six lucky landing Morobe Friday. Cessna
>
> damaged passengers survived without injury. flight
>
> Wau Garaina Civil Aviation yesterday
>
> safety department find out cause.

1 What crashed?
2 When did it happen?
3 How many passengers were there?
4 Were they badly hurt?
5 Where were they going?
6 What is the safety department going to do?

Scanning

Another way you can read quickly is to learn how to scan. Scanning is like skimming because you do not try to read all the words on a page.

- In skimming you look for information about a topic.
- In scanning you look for one special piece of information, such as the date someone was born.

How do you scan?

1 What are you looking for? It helps if you have a picture in your mind of the kind of information you are going to find.

Example 1

If you are looking for the year Papua New Guinea got self-government, you look for *numbers which are a date*: 1973.

Example 2

If you are looking for the percentage of how many people in Papua New Guinea can read and write, you look for a *number which is a percentage*: 48% (in 1996)

Example 3

If you want to know what day of the year Independence Day is celebrated you look for a date: *16 September*.

2 When you find some information that looks like what you are looking for, you have to read the other words around the information.

3 Then you can decide if it is the information that you want.

4 You need look only for the information you want. Keep the picture of the information clearly in your mind.

5 Do not start to read about other things that interest you.

Activity D

Try these questions. Think what you would need to see in your mind to be to find out these things. (You do not need to find the answer to the question.):

1. Where was Sir Michael Somare born?
2. What percentage of the population lives in rural areas?
3. What countries share borders with PNG?
4. What colours are on the American flag?
5. Who is the present Governor General of PNG?
6. What day of the year is Remembrance Day celebrated on?
7. What year was our constitution amended to have provincial government?
8. Which province is Ok Tedi located in?
9. How many motor vehicles are registered in PNG?
10. What is the height of the highest mountain in PNG?

Activity E

Do not read the passage below. Your eyes should move quickly over the lines of words and only stop when they come to something that could be the answer to the question. Follow these steps:

1 Read one question at a time.

2 Form a picture in your mind of what the answer looks like.

3 Move your eyes quickly over the passage.

4 When you come to what you think is the answer, stop and check it.

5 You might have to read a line to check if it is the answer you are looking for.

Questions:

1 Where was coffee first grown?

2 Which countries also grow coffee?

The history of coffee

Coffee has a very long history. It was first used as a food, then later as a medicine. Now it is popular as a hot drink. Coffee was first grown in North Africa. Today coffee is still grown in North Africa, but it is also grown in Java, India, Brazil and Papua New Guinea.

Thinking ahead when you are reading

When you read, your brain often guesses what words are coming. This is a useful skill to practise. It is called *predicting*.

Activity A

Practise doing the following with the book that you are reading: when you get to the bottom of a page, predict what the next word in the sentence will be. Turn the page and see if you are right.

Activity B

Look at this sentence with a missing word:

> What is a tsunami? A **t**_____________ is a very large sea wave caused by earthquakes or volcanoes erupting.

Did you say the missing word was **tsunami**? If you did, you predicted correctly.

Now try with these sentences. Write the sentence with the missing word.

1. Tsunamis happen at sea. When there is a tsunami, the **s**_________ rises and falls like a wave.
2. Tsunamis can cause damage on the coast. When the tsunami reaches the **c**___________, it can do two things.
3. The Tsunami can make the sea **r**_________ and fall or it can break like a wave.
4. If the sea gets shallow quickly close to the **c**___________, the sea will rise and fall.

5 If the sea does not get shallow quickly the **t**__________ can break like a wave.

6 The **w**__________ can cause a lot of damage.

Activity C

Here is a longer passage to practise prediction on.

Follow these steps:

1 Read the sentence and think about what might happen next.

2 Use the question to help you.

3 Do *not* read ahead at this stage. Use a piece of paper to *cover the answer until you write your prediction.*

4 Now you can uncover the text and check how well you predicted what would happen next. You do not need to have written exactly the same words as the answer.

A Story of the Aitape Tsunami

On the afternoon of 17 July, David Monana was sitting on a tractor near the church when he felt a big earthquake. The earthquake broke the statues of Mary in front of …

Prediction: (in front of what building?)

Answer:(the village church)

… the church David called out to Father Otton to come and look at …

Prediction (What did David want Father Otton to look at?)

Answer: (the damage that had been done to the statues by the earthquake)

... the damage. Father Otton walked to look at the damage, then returned to his house. After a while he heard a strange noise coming from the direction of the sea. He wanted to find out what the noise was, so he began to walk towards ...

Prediction: (where did he begin to walk towards?)

Answer: (the beach)

... the beach to find out what had caused the noise. He was met by his catechist. The catechist had seen the wave coming towards the beach. He was running very fast and calling out ...

Prediction: (what would he call out?)

Answer: (that there was a big wave coming and that they should run away)

... to Father Otton to run because there was a big wave coming towards the beach. Together they ran ...

Prediction: (where would they run to?)

Answer: (they ran away from the beach)

... away from the beach, towards the boat landing on the lagoon behind the village.

They reached the boat landing and stopped there. Behind them the water from the big wave ...

Prediction: (what damage would a very big wave or tsunami do to the village?)

Answer: (it went all through the village and broke the houses)

... swept through the mission station and the village and carried all the broken buildings and the tractor along with it.

Luckily, the water from the big wave slowed down before it reached David and Father Otton. The water then started to go back to ...

Prediction: (where would the sea water go back to?)

Answer: (to the sea)

... the sea. The group of people at the boat landing were safe, but many others were killed.

The information about Tsunamis comes from Professor Hugh Davies of UPNG.

Unit 7

What to do when you don't know some words

Sometimes when you are reading, you find words that you do not know the meaning of. What do you do? Follow these steps:

1 Look at how the word is used in the sentence. Is it a name of something (noun), is the word telling about an action or something that is happening (verb)? Does the word describe something (adjective) or tell how an action is being done (adverb)?
2 Look to see if there is another word nearby, or part of the sentence nearby, which tells you anything about the unknown word.
3 Look at the other words in the sentence and see how the unknown word fits in.
4 If you cannot find out the meaning this way, then use your dictionary.

Example:

Finding out the meaning of the underlined word, in the following sentence.

The most amazing and frightening thing that happened in those years was the *unexpected* sight of the first planes to fly over our valley.

What was the unexpected sight? (the planes)

How did the author feel about it? (amazed and frightened)

You can say that something is unexpected if it is new and amazing or frightening.

Activity A

Do not use a dictionary for this exercise. Read the passage and then match the words on the following list with their meanings.

When Papua New Guineans first saw planes flying in PNG, some of them ran away into hiding and others thought they were big birds and tried unsuccessfully to shoot them down. Later, air transport was used intensively with the discovery of gold in the Wau Valley in Morobe Province in the 1920s.

hiding	failed to do what they wanted
unsuccessfully	finding
transport	a place where they were hidden
intensively	way of carrying goods
discovery	many times

Activity B

Work out the meanings of the underlined words in the passage. Write a list of the words and their meanings.

During the Second World War, there were about sixty aerodromes built in Papua New Guinea. Air transport has now become an important mode of transport in modern Papua New Guinea. With the absence of a good road network, many people in remote villages need air transport to reach the outside world. In addition to the major aerodromes such as Lae and Port Moresby, there are about 459 other aerodromes mostly operated by the private sector, such as mission churches. The vast majority of these are grass-surfaced runways.

Unit 8

Words that stand in for other words

Read these sentences:

When Kerava saw Kerava's friend last night, Kerava's friend gave Kerava a present.

When Kerava saw her friend last night, her friend gave her a present.

Both of these sentences have the same meaning.

In the first sentence, Kerava's name is repeated three times. This makes the sentence look funny when you read it. In the second sentence, Kerava's name is only written once. For the other three times, other words are put in the place of her name.

Writers do this so that the same words don't need to be repeated. When you are reading you need to understand what these other words mean.

Activity A

In the sentences about Kerava, a pronoun (her) was used instead of Kerava's name. Underline the other pronouns in this sentence:

When Kerava saw her friend last night, her friend gave her a present.

Now read the following sentences. The sentences are about some people who live near Ok Tedi. What word in each sentence is the pronoun being used for? Write the word.

1 The Wangbin people left *their* (Wangbin people's) traditional houses.

2 The Wangbin villagers moved into *their* (__________) new houses. The new houses are near Tabubil.

3 Their pigs were left behind because *they* (__________) do not like changes.

4 The pigs have caused a lot of problems. *They* (__________) have broken some fences.

5 The councillor has spoken to the owners of the pigs. *He* (__________) said the pigs would be shot.

Activity B

Look at these sentences:

I live in Lae. I have lived in Lae for ten years.

I live in Lae. I have lived there for ten years.

Now read the following sentences. What place in the sentence is the place word being used for? Write the word.

1 A man from Wangbin said his people do not want the pigs at their new village. But the pigs have gone *there* (__________) and left their droppings.

2 He said, "We do not want them *here* (__________), because this is a clean place."

3 At the new village the houses are made from permanent materials. The people have made new gardens *there* (__________).

4 At the old village the pigs have left their droppings on the ground near the houses. You can see the droppings *there* (__________).

5 A woman said that she liked the new village. She said, "*Here* (_______________) the ground around the houses is clean."

Activity C

Look at these sentences:

I moved to Lae in April. I have lived there since April.

I moved to Lae in April. I have lived there since <u>then</u>.

Now read the following sentences. What time name in the sentence is the time word being used for? Write the word.

1 The Wangbin people moved to the new village in 1996. Before *that time* (_______________) they lived in a traditional village.

2 The new houses were built in January. Since *then* (_______________) the people have been happy.

3 The Wangbin people held a meeting in August to talk about their pigs. At *that time* (_______________) the pigs were spoiling the new town.

4 In September they made some new rules about pigs in the town. Since *then* (_______________) some pigs have been shot.

5 In 1999 only three pigs were shot. At *that time* (_______________) most pigs were safe inside their fences.

Activity D

Write what words the pronouns, time words or place words are being used for:

1 Anna is a woman from Wangbin. Early each morning *she* (pronoun) gets up.

2 Anna lets out the pigs from *their* (pronoun) fence.

3 At 6 o 'clock her children get ready to go to school. *There* (place word) the children will learn information about hygiene and why pigs should not be kept near the houses.

4 In the afternoon the children come home. *Then* (time word) *they* (pronoun) help Anna feed the pigs.

5 Anna likes *her* (pronoun) new house very much.

6 Anna likes the new village. *She* (pronoun) thinks it is much better *there* (place word) than at the old village.

Unit 9

Words that join ideas

Words such as *and, however, as well as, therefore* and *but* are used in sentences and paragraphs. These words join ideas. Each of the joining words has a special meaning. You will understand more when you read, if you know what these joining words mean.

Activity A

Here are some joining words you often find when you are reading:

and, but, or, so, for

Underline the joining words in the sentences below. Look at how the joining words are used in these sentences. Then write your own sentence to follow the pattern:

1 Eat your rice and fish.

2 ______________________________

3 Playing basketball makes me tired but happy.

4 ______________________________

5 Do you want to play basketball or volleyball?

6 ______________________________

7 I felt tired, so I sat down to rest.

8 ______________________________

9 I got into trouble for being late again.

10 ______________________________

Activity B

Some joining words show that you are adding one idea to another idea. Read these sentences. Underline the joining words.

> Gure and Alice went to the trade-store. They bought a tin of fish and a packet of rice. When they got home they cooked some bananas and ibika. The food was tasty and hot. They served the food to their grandfather and grandmother.

Activity C

Write a paragraph of your own, like the paragraph in Activity B. Use the same joining words.

Activity D

Write the words that are joined in these sentences:

1 Do you like both ripe and green mangoes?

2 Do you like both dogs and cats?

3 Do you like to dive and swim?

4 Do you like him and her?

5 Do you like to write quickly and neatly?

Activity E

Some other words that add ideas are: *as well as* and *in addition.* Underline the joining words in the following sentences. Look at how the joining words are used in these sentences. Then write your own sentence to follow the pattern:

1 I like maths as well as English.

2 ______________________________

3 They bought some grease in addition to the flour their mother asked them to buy.

4 ______________________________

Activity F

Some joining words tell us that a *cause or reason* is in a sentence or paragraph. These are some of the words you will find when you are reading: *because, since, as.* Read these sentences. Underline the joining words.

> We were feeling sick yesterday because we ate too many green mangoes. My mother said to us that since we liked green mangoes so much we should help her. She told us to climb the tree and pick a lot of mangoes because she wanted to take them to the market. As we always do what our mother tells us, we climbed the tree. We didn't eat any more mangoes, because our stomachs were still sore from the day before.

Now answer these questions about the reasons and causes:

1 Why did the children feel sick? Because ...

2 Why did mother say they should help her? Because ...

3 Why did mother tell them to pick mangoes? Because ...

4 Why did they do what their mother said? Because ...

5 Why didn't they eat any more mangoes? Because ...

Activity G

Write reasons or causes for each of these sentences:

1 The class was unhappy because ________________ .

2 Since ________________________, I felt very hungry.

3 As ________________________, I could not do my work in class.

4 I enjoy playing near the river because ______________ .

5 I got into trouble as I __________________________ .

6 We were late back since __________________________ .

Activity H

Joining words such as *but, however* and *although* are used to show the reader that the next idea is *different* in some way.

Example:

I won the race, *although* I had a sore leg.

Why is the idea *different*? It seems *different* because you would expect that the sore leg would mean he would lose the race.

Read these sentences and see how the joining word is used. Underline the joining word. Write your own sentence following the pattern.

1 I like dogs, but this dog frightened me.

2 ______________________________

3 It looked like a beautiful day, however, I decided to carry my umbrella.

4 ______________________________

5 Although I had studied very hard, I did not get good marks in the test.

6 ______________________________

Unit 10

Finding causes and effects when reading

When you read, you need to be able to find what are the causes of things, and what are the effects. A *cause* is what makes something happen, or the reason for something. An *effect* is something that happens because of something else. Look out for words like: *as a result, because, this meant, the result.*

Activity A

Write answers to these questions about effects. Start each answer using the following pattern:

When you forget to water a young plant the effect is …

1 What happens when you forget to water a young plant?

2 What happens when you lose your exercise book?

3 What happens when you are late to school?

4 What happens to the river when it rains very hard?

5 What happens when you forget to put wood on the fire?

6 What happens when you don't wash your hands before you eat?

7 What happens when you talk in church?

8 What happens when you work very hard in class?

Activity B

Write answers to these questions about causes. Start each answer using the following pattern:

A baby cries because …

1 What makes a baby cry?
2 What makes a pot of water boil?
3 What makes a dog bark?
4 What makes your teacher happy?
5 What makes the trees move about?
6 What makes a puddle dry up?
7 What makes a torch stop shining?
8 What makes a person get sick from malaria?

Activity C

Read the following passage. Find the cause and effect sentences. Ask yourself: What was the cause, what was the effect? Then, fill in the following table:

It rained all week because it was the wet season. The wet season always happens in the school holidays. The result was the ground around our house was very wet by the end of the week. This meant we could not play our usual game of volleyball on the court near our house. I have a net on the platform under the house.

My cousins came after they had worked in the garden. We sat around a fire and roasted peanuts and talked for a while. Then my cousins were bored because they could not play. As a result we all decided to go to the river and float down on the flood. The river was running very fast. We used some banana stems that we cut from a garden on the river bank. My uncle was washing in the river. He saw what we were doing and got angry because we cut down some banana stems that he was saving for a big feast. As a result we all had to help him plant new bananas. We worked with my uncle for the rest of the holidays. That meant we had no time to play volleyball, even when the court dried up.

Cause	**Effect**
it was the wet season	*it rained all week*

Unit 11

Recognising time order in reading

Many stories or instructions you read are written in *sequence*. This means that they are written in the order that things happen.

Activity A

Read the following story and underline the words that show the order that things happen. Look out for words like: *first, second, third, next, after that, then, last(ly).*

Visit to a special place

Near our village there is a special waterfall. This waterfall is where some of our clan's spirits live. During the last school holidays, my grandfather decided it was time for me to go there.

First we had to cross the river. It had been raining, so we took some rubber tubes to help us. Then we walked through long grass for about fifteen minutes until we reached the bottom of the hills. After that, we followed a little river up into the hills. The bed of the river was very narrow and sometimes we had to hold onto tree roots, and pull ourselves along.

After about one and a half hours we could hear a roaring noise. Then my grandfather told us that we had to stop talking or the spirits would go away. Next we went around a bend in the river and there it was. The water fell over a cliff. It was very narrow. We were not allowed to swim in the pool at the bottom of the falls, because that is where the spirits live.

Then we sat down for a while, and after a few minutes some butterflies came and settled near us. Grandfather said they were a sign that the spirits were pleased to see us. Lastly we left some special bananas at the edge of the pool, and went home.

Activity B

Answer these questions about the order of events in the story.

1 What was the first thing that happened?
Grandfather ...
2 What was the second thing that happened?
3 What was the third thing that happened?
4 What was the fourth thing that happened?
5 What was the fifth thing that happened?
6 What was the sixth thing that happened?
7 What was the seventh thing that happened?
8 What was the eighth thing that happened?
9 What was the ninth thing that happened?
10 What was the tenth thing that happened?

Activity C

This story is muddled up. Use the sequence signals to help you put the sentences in the correct order. Then, write the story correctly.

Road-side market

We sell bags of peanuts at the side of the road. Then we put them into old flour bags. Lastly, we wait for someone to come and buy the bags of peanuts. Next we stack the bags at the side of the road. First we pull the peanuts out of the ground. Second we let them dry in the sun until the shells are hard. After that a tractor carries the bags to the road-side.

Activity D

You will find sequence words are used for instructions or descriptions of how to do something. Underline the sequence words in these instructions.

How to make a row of paper cats

Things you need:
scissors, pencil, paper
What to do:
First, cut a strip of paper 82 cm long and 15 cm wide.
Second, fold the paper over 10 cm from one end.
Third, turn the paper over and fold the end again
Keep doing this, turning the paper over each time, until all the paper is used up.

Next, use the pencil to draw a cat on the top fold. Make sure part of the cat touches the left and right edges of the folded paper.

Then, use the scissors to cut out the cat. Cut through all the folds. Be careful to leave some uncut edges on both sides of the paper.

Lastly, unfold the paper and you will see a row of cats. Colour them different colours.

Activity E

These instructions are not in order. Put them in the right order, then write them out like the instructions for Activity D.

How to make a tin can telephone

Things you need:

two washed tin cans (such as cans that have fin fish in them), five metres of string, hammer, nail, a friend

What to do:

Next, use the hammer and nail to make a hole in the middle of the bottom of each can.

After that, get your friend to hold one can and you hold the other can.

Now, do the same for the other can.

First, take the tops of the two cans off.

Lastly, get your friend to put the open end of their can up to their ear while you speak into the can. Move away from each other as far as the string will go. The sound of your voice will travel along the string to your friend's ear.

Then poke the strings through the bottom of the can from the outside and tie a knot on the inside of the can.

Unit 12

How to find facts and opinions when reading

Some things you read will try to persuade you. An advertisement will try to make you buy something by using special opinion words. A written opinion (such as a letter to the editor) will try to make you think the same way as the writer.

Activity A

Read this advertisement. There are some special opinion words in it that are used to persuade you. These words are underlined.

Activity B

Match the persuasive words with their correct meanings

Persuasive words	Meanings
ultimate travel experience	the very big and wonderful
cruise	very comfortable
luxurious	a comfortable, easy journey
cruising	the best ever holiday
the mighty	travelling easily and comfortably

Activity C

The MTS Discoverer advertisement also has facts. Find and write the facts. Answer the questions:

1 What is the name of the boat?

2 When is the boat going on the journey?

3 What seas is the boat visiting?

4 What islands is the boat visiting?

5 What river is the boat visiting?

Activity D

Here is another advertisement. Write the persuasive words. These are words that make the product sound good.

Activity E

Match the persuasive words with their correct meanings.

Persuasive words	Meanings
unique	the one you like the best
savoury	make something better
favourite	the only one of its kind
improve	very tasty

Activity F

Answer these questions about the facts in the advertisement. Be careful not to use persuasive words in your answer.

1 What can you do with *Maggi Seasoning*?

2 What two ways can you use it?

Activity G

Look through newspapers or magazines. Find examples of persuasive words used in advertisements. Write a list of as many persuasive words as you can find.

Activity H

Letters to the editor often give the writer's opinions (what someone believes). They also have facts (true things). Read this letter. Write answers to the questions. Use the underlined words to help you in your answers.

Stop rising prices

Please allow me to give my view about the rising price of goods.

On behalf of the citizens of this country, each day I see an increase in the price of goods. One toea or two toea is added to the normal price day by day.

The government spent K2.1 million to build the Boroko bus stop. Why not use that money to reduce the price of goods?

Are we trying to make our future generation into beggars on their own land?

Many of us don't earn much and the rising prices are adding to our burdens. I appeal to the Government leaders to look into this.

Concerned citizen, Port Moresby

1 Paragraph 1. What is the letter about? (fact)
2 Paragraph 2 Who is the writer making the complaint for? (opinion)
3 Paragraph 2 How often does the writer say this is happening? (opinion)
4 Paragraph 3 What does the writer complain about that the Government spent a lot of money on? (fact)
5 Paragraph 3 What does the writer say should be done with the money instead? (opinion)
6 Paragraph 3 What does the writer say may happen if the government doesn't do this? (opinion)

Activity I

Read this letter and write if the underlined parts are facts or opinions

Street sellers

I want to complain about street sellers.

1 There are street sellers near my house. 2. They sell betel nut and cigarettes.

The people who hang around these sellers 3. are looking to make trouble. 4. They are just there to rob people who walk along the road.

The sellers 5. do not clean up their stores. 6. There is a lot of bad smelling rubbish left around.

7. I am very angry about this. When is the Government going to do something to clean up the street sellers?

Anti-seller, Port Moresby

Unit 13

How to make notes and summaries

To make notes on a passage, you need to find the most important ideas first. Often, you find that the most important idea in a paragraph is in the first sentence.

Activity A

Here is some information about keeping your family healthy. Write the first sentence of each paragraph.

How to keep your family healthy

Many illnesses can be prevented by washing your hands with soap and water. You should wash your hands when you have been to the toilet, have been working in the garden, or before you touch food. Washing gets rid of the germs. Then the germs can't get onto food or into your mouth.

Illnesses can also be prevented by using proper latrines. Many illnesses, especially diarrhoea, come from the germs found in human faeces. People can swallow these germs if the germs get washed by rain into your water supply.

It is also important that you have a good water supply. Families that have a good, safe water supply don't get sick so often. A good, safe water supply should be far away from a latrine. The water supply should not be used by animals.

If you think your water supply is not good, you can prevent disease by boiling your water. Boiling water kills germs. It is especially important that you boil and cool water which is given to young children to drink. Young children can get sick from bad water more easily than adults.

You can also prevent illness by keeping your food in a safe and clean place. Germs can enter your body on food and make you sick. You can help by making sure food is very well cooked, especially meat, fish and chicken. You should eat food soon after it has been cooked so that it does not have time to go bad. Keep all of your food covered so that dust, flies and rats cannot put germs on it.

You should burn or bury any rubbish from your house. If you leave rubbish lying around, flies come and sit on it and then carry germs onto your food. Flies also like to breed in food scraps and vegetable and fruit peelings. If you just make a heap of these things near your house, you are helping the flies breed. Then the germs the flies carry will make you sick.

Activity B

Follow these steps to make the notes:

1 Write the title first: ____________________

2 Read the main sentence of the first paragraph. Pick out the important words. You do not need to write the whole sentence. Example: *wash hands with soap and water*

3 Write when you should wash your hands:
after________ after ________ before ________

4 Write why you do this:
gets ____________ germs can't ___________

5 Write the important words from the main sentence of the second paragraph: ____________________

6 Write why you should do this:
germs come from ________ germs can get into________

7 Write the important words from the main sentence of the third paragraph: ____________________

8 Why? ____________________________________

9 A good water supply is 1. _________ 2. ________

10 Write the important words from the main sentence of the fourth paragraph: ___________________________

11 Write why you should do this:

kills _______ young children get _________

12 Write the important words from the main sentence of the fifth paragraph: ___________________________

13 Say what you do:

cook _______eat _________keep ________

14 Write the important words from the main sentence of the sixth paragraph: ___________________________

15 Say why:

flies carry ___________flies breed ___________

Activity C

Read the passage *Animals that are hard to find* and look at the notes that follow. Look at the way the notes have been numbered. Look at the way some parts of the notes are close to the left margin and some are further in.

Animals that are hard to find

Introduction

Animals need to adapt to their environment if they are to stay alive. One problem they have is surviving predators, or other animals that want to eat them. When there are other species sharing their environment, some of them will be predators. Other animals will be prey, or the animals that the predators eat.

Many animals in the ocean escape their predators or hide themselves from their prey by disguising themselves, or making themselves look like something else.

Colour

Some fish disguise themselves from predators by hiding in coral, on the reef, where their colour stops other animals from seeing them.

The long-nose hawkfish has the same colour and pattern as a pink coral called sea fan.

The crocodile flathead is a predator. It lives close to the reef. It can make itself almost invisible because its colour is the same as the reef. It waits and pounces on passing prey.

Shape

Some fish disguise themselves by their shape. They hide by looking like something else.

The smooth flutemouth can grow as long as a metre, but it is very thin. When the ocean current moves, the fish looks like a stick being pushed around by the water. When the fish is among seaweed, it looks like seaweed. In this way it can hide itself from its prey and get a good meal.

The best animals at hiding are squid and octopus. They can change their colour very quickly to suit their background, and they can also change their shape.

Notes: Animals that are hard to find

I. need to adapt to environment

  A. fish disguise themselves to

    1. escape predators

    2. hide from prey

II. fish use colour to hide

  A. so that their predators can't see them

    1. the long-nose hawkfish

  B. so that their prey can't see them

    1. the Crocodile Flathead

III. fish use shape to hide

  A. they look like something else

    1. The Smooth Flutemouth

  B. they change shape

    1. squid and octopus

Activity D

Go back to the passage and underline the words that you can see in the notes on *Animals that are hard to find.*

Activity E

Use the following outline to write notes about the passage, *How to keep your family healthy* on page 42. The notes labelled *I, II* and *III* are the main points. The notes labelled *A, B* and *C* are the next most important notes. The notes labelled *1, 2,* and *3* are examples, or less important information.

Title: ______________________________

I. wash hands with soap and water

   A. after__________

   B. after __________

   C. before __________

      1. gets __________

      2. germs can't __________

II. ______________________________

   A. __________________

   B. __________________

III. ______________________________

A. ______________

1. ______________

2. ______________

IV. ______________________________

A. ______________

B. ______________

V. ______________________________

A. ______________

B. ______________

C. ______________

VI. ______________________________

A. ______________

B. ______________

Now you are ready to put the information in your own words when you do a project.

Unit 14

Improve your writing—step 1 brainstorming

Writing is hard work for everyone. But you can make the hard work easier by dividing the work into a number of steps. You can use these steps for any kind of writing. These steps will help you put down your ideas in an interesting and organised way.

Brainstorming

You already know a lot about many things. You already have some ideas about many things. Brainstorming means you bring these things out of your memory.

In brainstorming, these things are pulled out of your head and put down on paper, just as they come. This means your ideas won't be forgotten.

The topic you are given to write about, is the starting point for your brainstorming.

Activity A

Copy this example of some brainstorming ideas about the topic school libraries, and then add more ideas of your own. Sometimes one idea you write will remind you of something else. You can add examples to these ideas.

story books		catalogue
encyclopaedias	**School Libraries**	shelves
newspapers		projects

Activity B

Brainstorm the following topics:

- School subjects
- Cash crops
- Bride-price
- Traditional education (the education that happened before there were schools)

Activity C

The next step in brainstorming is to look at your page of ideas and see how some ideas belong together. Here are some brainstorming ideas about tourism in Papua New Guinea. See how some ideas belong together. Draw lines to join ideas that belong together:

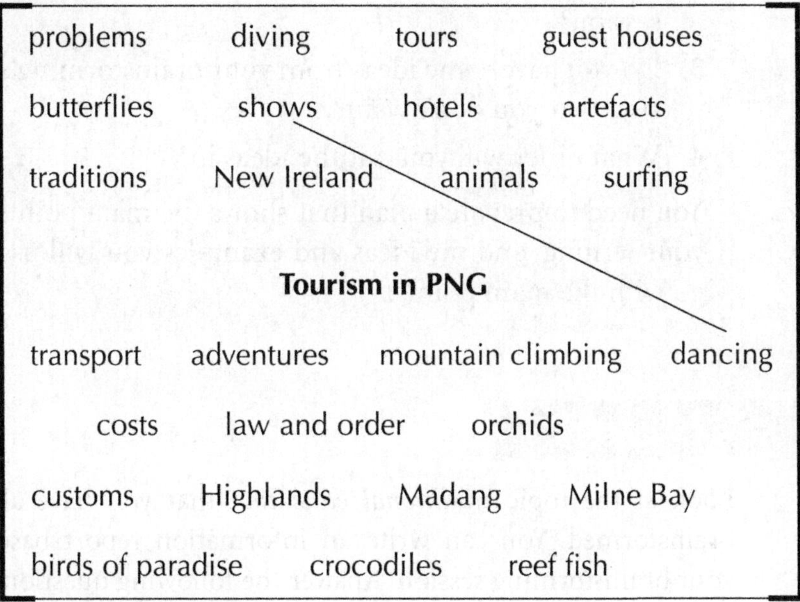

Activity D

Add some examples of your own to the brainstorming example on tourism in Papua New Guinea.

Unit 15

Improve your writing—step 2 planning

The next step is to decide how you are going to use the ideas you have put down on paper in your brainstorming session.

Things to think about:

1 What kind of writing are you doing? (telling a story, telling how to make something, giving information about something, explaining something, giving opinions)
2 Do you have enough ideas from your brainstorming session?
3 Do you have some ideas from your brainstorming session that you don't want?
4 What order will you put the ideas in?

You need to prepare a plan that shows the main points of your writing, and the ideas and examples you will use to go with the main points.

Activity A

Look at the topic *traditional education* that you have already brainstormed. You can write an information report based on your brainstorming session. Answer the following questions:

Traditional education in PNG

1 Would you need to write what traditional education is?
2 Why is this topic important?
3 Do you need to write about education today?
4 What are the main ideas you will use in the essay?
5 What are some of the examples you will use?

Activity B

Here is an outline. Use your ideas from your brainstorming session to fill in the spaces:

	Traditional education in Papua New Guinea
Explain the title (what the report is about and why it is important)	____________________ ____________________
The first idea you want to explain	____________________
An example of this idea	____________________
The second idea you want to explain	____________________
An example of this idea	____________________
The third idea you want to explain	____________________
An example of this idea	____________________
Summing up the report	____________________

Unit 16

Improve your writing—step 3 checking the first copy

The first draft of your essay is when you turn the main points and examples in your plan into sentences and paragraphs. Work quickly to get your ideas written. This is not your good copy. Later, you will read your copy again, several times, and change parts that need to be changed.

Activity A

Here is a plan for an opinion essay about tourism in Papua New Guinea. Use the plan to write your own sentences and paragraphs. Write your own examples:

Tourism in Papua New Guinea

Introduction

People come to countries like PNG to see new things

People come to countries like PNG to see the natural world.

Point of View: Tourism will bring problems for PNG

Paragraph 1. tourism costs a lot to build things tourists need
examples–hotels, roads, airports, water supply

Paragraph 2. tourists don't respect culture
examples–dances at shows are not for traditional purposes

Paragraph 3. culture is changed
examples–tourists buy and take away important objects, important objects lose traditional value when made to get money from tourists

Paragraph 4. tourists can cause damage to the environment
example–too many people will frighten wild animals

Conclusion: tourism can bring in money, give employment, but the number of tourist who come should be kept to a few.

Activity B

When you finish writing your first copy, you should leave it for a while. Check your first copy of the essay on tourism. It is a good idea to work with *a partner* to do the checking.

Stage 1 checking the information in the writing

Ask these questions:

- Is the information correct?
- Have I put enough information in?
- Have I put in information that is not part of the topic?

Look at the way you have written the information. Ask these questions:

- Are my ideas written in paragraphs?
- Are the paragraphs in the right order?
- Is the idea of each paragraph clear?
- Have I used connecting words to show how my paragraphs are linked?

Stage 2 checking the spelling and sentences

Ask these questions:

- Are my sentences proper sentences?
- Could some short sentences be joined? Are some sentences too long?
- Is my spelling and punctuation correct?

The final step is to write a good copy for other people to read.

Unit 17

Writing good paragraphs

You need to use paragraphs when you are writing stories, information reports, descriptions, explanations and discussions. A paragraph is a group of sentences about one main idea.

Activity A

Each paragraph has one main idea. All the sentences in the paragraph are about that one main idea. Read these paragraphs There is one sentence in each that should not be there. Find the sentence and write it down.

1 The rain continued all day. Gabi sat under his house and stared at the falling drops. He was thirteen years old. All his plans for going fishing in the river were spoilt.

2 The sports day arrived at last. Leilani had been practising the high jump all week. She had reached higher than she had ever reached before. Her mother works at the bank. She felt ready for the event.

3 Bees live in colonies called hives. A bee-hive may have up to 50 000 bees. The bees make honey to feed their young. I love honey.

4 Glaciers move at different speeds. The glaciers in the Himalayan Mountains are longer than the glaciers in Switzerland. One glacier in the Swiss Alps moves two and a half centimetres an hour in summer. In Greenland, some glaciers can move up to eighteen metres a day.

5 Butterflies have to go through four stages of life before they become adults. The stages are egg, caterpillar, pupa and butterfly. Butterflies can be very beautiful. At each stage they change size shape and colour.

Activity B

A good way for you to write a paragraph is to write the most general sentence first. The sentences after the most general sentence explain that sentence.

The sentences in the following paragraphs are out of order. Put them in order and then write the paragraph by following the outline:

1 They do a lot of work in the hive. For example, they guard the hive, build the honeycomb, clean the empty cells and take care of the young bees. Female bees are called workers.

Main sentence:
More about the main sentence:
Example:

2 Carnivorous plants make food in their leaves, but they also eat insects and small animals. For example, the Venus fly trap uses a spring-trap to catch its prey. They have leaves that are like traps.

Main sentence:
More about the main sentence:
Example:

Activity C

The following sentences can be put into three different groups. Find the four sentences that belong together, and write them as a paragraph.

Often they speak Tok Pisin.

A young boy climbs the banana plant.

Sometimes they speak English at home with their parents.

The clay for the pots comes from the mountain behind the village.

When bananas are nearly ready, they are wrapped.

It is important to keep the clan language alive, because it is part of the clan culture.

The bunch stays wrapped until it is ready to be eaten.

First women go in groups to get the clay.

Then they get the clay ready.

Next the men make the pots.

He uses dead banana leaves to wrap the banana bunch.

Children who grow up in town might not speak their clan's language.

Activity D

1 The opening sentence gives the main idea of the paragraph.

2 Other sentences give details and examples that belong with the main idea.

3 The last sentence pulls the ideas in the paragraph together.

Use the following sample paragraph as a guide to writing your own paragraph about an activity you enjoy.

I like visiting Lae because there are lots of interesting things to do. You can go shopping. The market is also fun to visit. You can go to the botanical gardens and see some interesting plants. You can go to the Rainforest Habitat and see some animals and birds. At Voco Point you can watch the boats bringing people to Lae. It would be hard to get bored in Lae.

Activity E

Here are some ideas for paragraphs about traditional food. You are given part of the first sentence of each paragraph. Write the paragraph with details.

Example:

Main idea: Most people know how to make the traditional food of their area.

Details: The traditional food is based on the kind of crops they can grow. Different crops grow in different climates. Bananas are often grown near the coast. Kaukau is often grown in the Highlands.

1 *Main idea*: The main food crop in my area is ...

Details: It is grown ... We pick it when ...

2 *Main idea*: This food is cooked by ...

Details:

3 *Main idea*: On special feasts we ...

Details:

Unit 18

Paragraphs in different kinds of writing

Paragraphs help the reader understand a piece of writing. When you write a paragraph you organise your ideas. Each new paragraph has a different main point.

Activity A

Read the following information passage about ants. Complete the table by writing which main point belongs with which paragraph:

Main idea	Paragraph
Ants' bodies	
How ants find their way	
Introducing ants–what are they?	
Ants' nests	

Ants

1 Ants are insects with six legs. There are many different kinds of ants. They are different in colour, different in size, and live in different environments. However, they all have some things which are the same.

2 Ants have bodies which are in three parts. The skeleton of the ant is on the outside. All ants have a head, an abdomen and a thorax. They have six legs, two eyes, and two feelers.

3 Ants live together in large nests. One ant is called the queen. She lays the eggs for the whole nest. She is looked after by worker ants. These ants are very strong.

4 Ants find their way by patterns of light. They also have special sense organs in the joint of their legs. They can follow chemical trails which they leave between the nest and where their food is.

Activity B

A new paragraph in an information report gives more information. Each paragraph gives different pieces of information about the topic. The first sentence of the paragraph tells you what is the new fact for the paragraph.

Follow this outline and write an information report on an animal you know:

Title:

Introducing the animal–what is it?

What it looks like

What it does

Anything special about it

Activity C

You also use paragraphs when you write a discussion. You write a new paragraph in a discussion when you write a new point, or when you change from looking at things in favour of your point of view, to things against your point of view.

Following is part of a discussion, but the paragraph breaks have been left out. Find the paragraph breaks. Look for an introduction, some points in favour of longer library hours, and some points against longer library hours. Write the discussion with the paragraph breaks put in. Follow the outline.

Longer library hours

Many schools have libraries but the libraries are shut a lot of the time. A lot of students think that school libraries should be open for a longer time. Firstly, the library should be open for longer hours because many students do not have books at home which they can use. The longer hours would mean they could go to the library after school and use the books to complete homework or find out things for projects. For example, most people don't have encyclopaedias and students need to use them in the library. As well as providing books, longer library hours would help students who do not have a good place to study at home. Many students live in houses where there are a lot of other family members. The family might not understand that students need a quiet place to study. On the other hand, the librarians would have to work longer hours. This may not suit them, as they have their own families to look after. They would have to make arrangements for child-care, and this costs money, so the school might have to pay them more. The school would also have to pay more for electricity if the library was open at night. The school might not have enough money in the budget to pay the extra amount. There are some points in favour of longer library hours, and some point against longer library hours

Introduction–what is the topic?

First paragraph in favour of longer hours

Second paragraph in favour of longer library hours

First point against longer library hours

Second point against longer library hours

Summing up

Activity D

When you write a new description, you should make a new paragraph. Examples:

1 when you change from looking at something from a distance to looking at it close up

2 when you write about a change in time

3 when you write about a change in mood, such as happy to sad

Follow this outline and write some paragraphs about walking through a food garden.

> Where is the food garden and what does it look like from a distance?
>
> When you get close, what is the first thing you see?
>
> If you bend down to the ground, what do you see?
>
> What insects or birds are flying around?
>
> What is the garden like in the morning?
>
> What is the garden like in the evening?
>
> What makes you feel unhappy about the garden?
>
> What makes you feel good about the garden?

Activity E

Longer pieces of writing often have a paragraph at the start, called the introduction, and a paragraph at the end, called the conclusion. Important points:

1 The introduction must be linked to the topic.

2 You explain the topic, or give your point of view.

3 Conclusions are short.

4 You write a summary only if your writing is very long.

5 You do not put in any new information or examples in a conclusion.

Unit 19

Adding details

A paragraph begins with a main idea. The main idea is followed by details. The kind of details you will put in the paragraph will depend on the kind of writing.

Activity A

When you are doing *creative writing*, you need details to make the writing more interesting. Here is a story without details. It is very boring. Make the story exciting. Decide where you will break for paragraphs and add details of your own:

> The two girls were in the bus. The bus reached the bus stop. They got down. They could see their home in the distance. They started walking towards their house. They walked through the trees. They saw their mother waving to them. They ran towards her. Their mother said hello. They went inside the house.

Activity B

When you are doing *descriptive writing*, the details help you explain and describe the topic. Read these descriptive paragraphs about agriculture in the Markham Valley. Then write similar paragraphs about your own agriculture.

> The main food crops grown by the people of the Markham Valley are bananas. This starchy plant is their staple food. A garden might begin by being planted with beans and ibika, but soon you will see that the bananas are growing. All over the landscape you will see large groups of bananas which is the basis of a family's food supply.

There are many kinds of banana. Some are short and have a thick skin. Some are longer. Some plants grow very tall, while others are quite short. The different kinds all have their own names, and some have special purposes, such as for exchange with relatives or for special feast days. Some, such as *zerab*, cannot be sold, for fear that the buyer will put salt on them, and this will spoil future crops.

Activity C

When you are preparing *discussion writing*, you write details to help you persuade your reader that you have a strong point of view. Each paragraph should start by saying your main idea statement again. Here is an outline. Write the first sentence for each paragraph outline given below, following the pattern:

Main idea statement: We should get rid of the laws against street selling.

Pattern: The first (second/third/next) reason why (put your main idea here) ________________ is because________________

Example:

Paragraph 1

<u>The first reason why</u> we should get rid of the laws against street selling <u>is because</u> the police do not use the laws.

Paragraph 2

because many people use the money they make to pay for school fees

Paragraph 3

because there is a lot of unemployment and this is something for people to do

Paragraph 4

because it provides a market for small producers

Unit 20

Getting ready for exams

If you want to do well in exams, you have to think about getting ready before you sit exams.

Activity A

You can learn to use your time well. The following checklist is about how well you are using your time right now. Write *yes* or *no* after each question:

1. Do I waste a lot of time doing things which are not important, such as sitting and thinking about failing instead of starting to study?
2. Do I make a plan for times to study?
3. Do I know how to pick out main points in my notes and textbooks?
4. Do I know how to make summaries of my notes and textbooks?
5. Do I leave enough time to go over my work for big exams?
6. Can I sit still in my study place for one hour at a time?
7. Do I start doing my work, but stop before I finish it?

Activity B

1. Draw up a plan for one whole term.
2. Put a red border around the exam dates.
3. Draw a line in front of each exam date to show how long you think you need to prepare for the exam.

Example:

Weeks	1 2 3 4 5 6 7 8 9 10 11 12 13 14
Maths	——————→ Exam
English	————→ Exam
SS	——————————→ Exam
Science	——————————————→ Exam

Activity C

Make a daily work plan:

1 Write a list of the things you need to do (including any other school work you have to do).

2 Now put the list in order, with the most important work first.

3 Put some details about each task, so you can see exactly what you have to do.

4 Work out how much time you think each task will take.

5 Put a column where you can tick ✓ when you finish each task.

- You can study better on some days than others. Use those days for doing difficult tasks.
- Be sure to allow time for writing a summary of the work you have done that day. You can keep these summaries in a special revision exercise book.

Activity D

Do you find it hard to get yourself started on study? Do you find it hard to concentrate? Answer these questions about getting started.

1 Do I hate sitting at my desk or study place?
2 When I'm at my desk do I sit and dream instead of starting?
3 Does feeling that I have to study make me feel uncomfortable?
4 Do I keep putting off starting on revision?
5 Do I get restless when I'm sitting at my desk?

Activity E

Ideas to help you get started on study. Do these things now:

1 Put a big tick ✓ in the space on your daily plan, when you finish a task.
2 Divide your tasks up into smaller units that you can do.
3 Don't make any task so big that you can't do it or finish it in an hour.
4 Take regular breaks—give your mind a rest for a few minutes each hour.
5 Give yourself a reward when you finish what you set out to do. (e.g. if I finish all my tasks, I can go and play basketball.)

6 Look into the future—find out more about what you want to do with your life after the exam, so that you know what you are aiming for.
7 Study with a friend—test each other, make summaries for your partner and discuss them.

Activity F

Answer the following questions:

1 Are you usually tired when you study?

2 Is there a lot of noise in your study area?

3 Are you happy when your friends interrupt you?

4 Does your mind wander away from the task?

If you answer *yes* for questions 1 and 2, you can take steps yourself to overcome these problems by making changes in your life and environment. Do this now:

1 Study at the time of the day when you feel really awake.

2 Find a quieter place to study.

If you answer *yes* for questions 3 and 4, try doing these things:

1 Politely ask your friends not to interrupt you, when you are studying.

2 Stretch your mind—make summaries and lists. Use these like warm-up exercises for the mind.

3 Set yourself a goal to reach. Ask yourself a question about your study and find the answer.

4 Take breaks—these help concentration as well as keeping you going.

5 When you read for revision, keep a pencil in your hand. Underline, highlight and write names, main points and figures on scrap paper.

Unit 21

In the exam

Exams are to find out how much you have understood what has been taught in a subject. If you have prepared well, you should get good marks.

Activity A

Answer these question about the last time you sat an exam:

1 Did you make sure you woke up in time?

2 Did you have some breakfast?

3 Did you know exactly where the exam was to be held?

4 Did you know exactly when you had to get to the exam room and when the exam started?

5 Did you choose a seat that suited you? (At the front? Out of the sun?)

6 Did you take time to fill in the front (identification) page properly?

7 Did you use the reading time wisely, or spend it looking round at your friends?

8 Did you plan how much time to spend on each section or answer before you started to write?

9 Did you write neatly?

10 Did you leave time to check your paper near the end of the exam?

If you answered any questions with a *no*, then you will have to work to change yourself.

Activity B

You usually know how long the exam will take. Sometimes you will be told how many questions there will be, and how many marks each question is worth before the exam. Follow these steps:

1 Give yourself enough time to read the exam paper right through. Sometimes you will be given reading time before the exam starts. If you are not given reading time, then give part of the total time to reading.

2 Use the reading time to think about which question to answer if there is a choice.

3 Give yourself the right amount of time to answer every question you have to answer. You can work this out as follows: Divide the time by looking at the marks for each question.

Example: 2 hour exam:

120 minutes, less ten minutes at beginning and ten minutes at the end. This gives you 100 minutes for the exam itself. If the questions have equal value, divide by the number of questions and work out how long to spend on each question. Draw up a plan to show what time you should finish one question and go on to the next question.

KEEP TO YOUR TIME PLAN.

If the questions are not equal value, you need to spend more time on those questions that are worth more marks. Example: Q1 10 marks, Q2 20 marks, Q3 20 marks, Q4 50 marks. You would spend more time on Q4, and less time on Q1.

Try these:

1 Which question would you spend the most time on?
Question 1 (30 marks)
Question 2 (10 marks)
Question 3 (10 marks)

2 Which question would you spend the most time on?
Question 1 (10 marks)
Question 2 (20 marks)
Question 3 (15 marks)
Question 4 (10 marks)

Remember to give yourself enough time at the end of the exam to go over your whole paper. Check on your answers and correct any wrong sentences and spelling.

Activity C

Why are some questions worth more than others? This is because you are expected to write more about some questions than others. If one question is worth ten marks and one is worth twenty, you are expected to write more information for the question worth twenty marks. As the markers read your answer, they will be looking for things to tick. Make sure you write all of the important points you need for your answer.

Activity D

When answering *short answer exams*:

1 Read the question carefully. Look for the important words.
2 Write what you are asked for: a list, a sentence or a paragraph.

Activity E

When answering *multiple choice exams*:

1 Fill in all the answer spaces.
2 Make any changes clear.
3 Do not mark two answers.
4 Do the easy questions first.
5 Look out for key words like *always, all, many, best.*
6 Give yourself time to check when you have finished.

Activity F

When answering *essay exams*:

1 Underline the most important words in the essay question. They will tell you what kind of answer you should write. Try this:

Describe a rural society you know. (10 marks)

2 Make sure you know what the most important words mean. Try these:

Compare the farming methods of the highlands with the farming methods of the coast. (10 marks) What does *compare* mean?

Discuss the reasons why we need to keep our forests safe. (20 marks) What does *discuss* mean?

3 Follow the steps for essay writing. Start with brainstorming. Check your essay.

4 Focus on the key points you have underlined. What would these be in the questions above (Question 2)?

Answers

Unit 2 Finding words quickly

E 1. button 2. insist 3. pebble 4. region 5. struggle

Unit 3 Using the dictionary

(Answers to B, C, D may vary with different dictionaries.)

A beaker–cup, bungalow–house, elastic–stretch, hour-glass–time, nil–nothing, squander–waste

B ash–2, egg–2, fuse–2, refuse–2, row–3, scuttle–2, set–2, till–3, utter–2, will–2

C bind–4, bug–4, hop–3, horn–3, range–7, stack–3, test–3, warm–3, write–3, X-ray–2

D 1. The doctor–**2** Papua New Guinea–**3** The teacher–**1**
2. The football player–**4** The guard outside–**2**
The market seller –**1** The guards stood–**3**

Unit 5 Reading quickly—skimming and scanning

C 1. Cessna plane 2. Friday 3. six 4. no 5. Wau to Garaina 6. find out what caused the crash

D 1. place name 2. percentage number 3. names of countries 4. colours 5. name with Sir 6. date with month and day number 7. year date 8. province name 9. number 10. number with 'm' for metres.

Unit 6 Thinking ahead when you are reading

B 1. sea 2. coast 3. rise 4. coast 5. tsunami 6. wave

Unit 7 What to do when you don't know some words

A hiding–place where they were hidden, unsuccessfully–not doing what they wanted, transport–way of carrying goods, intensively–many times, discovery– finding

Unit 8 Words that stand in for other words

A 2. Wangbin villagers' 3. pigs 4. pigs 5. the councillor

B 1. the new village 2. the new village 3. the new village 4. in the old village near the houses 5. the new village

C 1. 1966 2. January 3. August 4. September 5. 1999

D 1. she→Anna 2. their→pigs 3. there→ school
4. then→afternoon, they→the children 5. her→Anna
6. she→Anna, there→new village

Unit 9 Words which join ideas

A 1. and, 3. but, 5. or, 7. so, 9. for

B all are *and*

D 1. ripe and green mangoes 2. dogs and cats 3. dive and swim 4. him and her 5. quickly and neatly

E 1. as well as 2. in addition to

F because, since, because, as, because 1. Because they ate green mangoes 2. because they liked green mangoes so much
3. because she wanted to take them to the market
4. because they always do 5. because their stomachs were still sore

H 1. but 3. however 5. although

Unit 10 Finding causes and effects when reading

C It had rained all week because … The result was the ground … This meant we could not play … Then my cousins were bored because … As a result we all decided … and got angry because we cut down … As a result we all … That meant we had no time …

Cause	Effect
it was the wet season	it rained all week
it rained all week	the ground was wet
the ground was wet	we could not play volleyball
we could not play	my cousins were bored
we were bored	we went to the river
we cut banana stems	uncle got angry
uncle got angry	help him
help him	no time to play

Unit 11 Recognising time order in reading

A first, then, after that, after about one and a half hours, then, next, then, after a few minutes, lastly

B 1. Grandfather decided it was time for us to go to the waterfall. 2. … cross the river 3. … walked through the long grass 4. … a little river up into the hills 5. … could hear a roaring noise 6. … stop talking 7. … went around a bend in the river 8. … water fell over a cliff 9. … butterflies settled near us 10. left special bananas at the edge of the pool

C We sell … First we pull … Second we let … Then we put … After that a tractor … Next we stack … Lastly we wait …

D first, second, third, next, then, lastly

E First take the tops … Next use the hammer … Then poke the strings … Now do the same … After that get your … Lastly get your friend …

Unit 12 How to find facts and opinions when reading

B ultimate travel experience—the best ever holiday; cruise—a comfortable, easy journey; luxurious—very comfortable; cruising—travelling easily and comfortably; the mighty—the very big and wonderful

C 1. MTS Discoverer 2. Christmas, New Year 3. Coral, Solomon, Bismarck 4. Islands of Milne Bay, Morobe and Madang 5. Sepik

D unique savoury, favourite, improve

E unique—the only one of its kind, savoury—very tasty, favourite—the one you like the best, improve—make something better

F 1. Put it on your food 2. marinade, improve taste

H 1. price of goods 2. citizens of PNG 3. day by day 4. bus stops 5. reduce prices 6. make future generation into beggars

I 1. fact 2. fact 3. opinion 4. opinion 5. opinion 6. opinion 7. fact

Unit 13 How to make notes and summaries

E Title: Family health

I. wash hands with soap and water
   A. after toilet
   B. after garden
   C. before food
      1. gets rid of germs
      2. germs can't get onto food, in mouth

II. use proper latrines
   A. diarrhoea from germs in human faeces
   B. germs in water supply

III. good water supply
   A. don't get sick so often
      1. away from latrine
      2. not used by animals

IV. improve water supply
   A. boil water
   B. children can get sick

V. food in safe, clean place
   A. cook well
   B. eat soon
   C. keep covered

VI. remove rubbish
   A. flies bring germs from rubbish
   B. flies breed in rubbish

Unit 17 Writing good paragraphs

A 1. He was thirteen years old 2. Her mother works in the bank 3. I love honey 4. The glaciers in the Himalayan … 5. Butterflies can be very beautiful

B 1. Female bees are called workers. They do a lot of work in the hive. For example … 2. Carnivorous plants make food in their leaves … They have leaves like … For example …

C When bananas are nearly ready, they are wrapped. A young boy climbs the banana plant. He uses dead banana leaves to wrap the banana bunch. The bunch stays wrapped until it is ready to be eaten.

Children who grow up in town might not speak their clan's language. Often they speak Tok Pisin. Sometimes they speak English at home with their parents. It is important to keep the clan language alive, because it is part of the clan culture.

The clay for the pots comes from the mountain behind the village. First women go in groups to get the clay. Then they get the clay ready. Next the men make the pots.

Unit 18 Paragraphs in different kinds of writing

A Ants' bodies 2; How ants find their way 4; introducing ants 1; ants' nests 3

C Many schools … Firstly the library … As well as providing books, longer library … On the other hand the librarians … There are some points …

Unit 19 Adding details

C Paragraph 2 The second reason why we should get rid of the laws against street selling is because many people use money from selling to pay for school fees.
Paragraph 3 The third reason why we should get rid of the laws against street selling is because there is a lot of unemployment and this is something for people to do.
Paragraph 4 The last reason why we should get rid of the laws against street selling is because it provides a market for small producers.

Unit 21 In the exam

B 1. Question 1 2. Question 2